They Called Her Rebel

True Stories of Warriors
Who Changed the World

ATHENA IVES

They Called Her Rebel: True Stories of Warriors Who Changed the World
© 2025 by **Dr. Athena Ives**

Published by **Lioness Press**
Arlington, Virginia
Hardback ISBN: **978-0-9980417-5-9**
eBook ISBN: **978-0-9980417-6-6**
Cover and interior artwork created using AI technology by **Dr. Athena Ives**
Printed in the United States of America
First Edition, 2025

Author's Note & Historical Disclaimer

This book is a tribute to the brave women that shaped history, often in the shadows or margins of written records. Every effort has been made to ensure the stories within are as historically accurate as possible. However, due to the limited documentation and the passage of time, some accounts blend recorded history with oral tradition, cultural memory, or legend. Where exact details are unavailable, the narrative honors the spirit and truth of their impact.

The illustrations throughout this book were created using artificial intelligence (AI) tools. Every effort was made to ensure that these visuals are culturally respectful, historically informed, and contextually appropriate (with a spark of magic) to reflect the legendary spirit of these women warriors. These images are not photographs or exact historical recreations, but imaginative representations intended to inspire, educate, and honor their legacies.

These pages are a reclamation-an effort to restore the presence and power of women whose stories deserve to be remembered. Where fact ends and legend begins, one thing remains clear: these women left their marks.

To all the little girls who grew up without a storybook like this.

For the ones who dreamed of being Mulan or Merida, only to be told they were fiction.

This book is for the girls who colored outside the lines, who questioned the rules, and who imagined themselves not in ball gowns but in boots, armor, and battle braids.

For the daughters who never saw themselves in the pages of history books. For the silenced and forgotten.

For the warrior women I served beside in combat.

For the Lionesses, CSTs, and FETs who carried the weight of the mission and one another.

A special thank you to Jax and Heidi, who reignited my spark and continue to blaze paths forward as fierce advocates for women in special operations.

This is for you. and this is for her, the one still rising.

Contents

Queen Artemisia I

The Queen Who Commanded Kings

The Greco-Persian Wars (480 BCE)

OVER 2,500 YEARS ago, during the great clash between the Persian Empire and the city-states of Greece, one of King Xerxes' boldest naval commanders was not a man but a queen. Artemisia [ahr-tuh-MEE-zhuh] I of Caria ruled the city of Halicarnassus, in what is now Turkey. When her husband died, she became regent for her young son. Artemisia wasn't content to rule from a throne.

When King Xerxes called for war, she answered-with ships, warriors, and a mind built for battle. Though she commanded only five of the 70 ships in Xerxes' vast navy, her fleet stood out. Artemisia became known for sharp strategy, calm leadership, and fearless decisions, earning respect from both Persian allies and Greek enemies. The Greek historian Herodotus wrote: "None of Xerxes' allies gave him better advice than Artemisia. It is remarkable that a woman took part in the war and led so well."

During the famous Battle of Salamis, the Persian fleet faced disaster. Greek ships, smaller but faster, trapped Xerxes' armada in the narrow straits. As panic spread among the Persians, Artemisia remained steady. Surrounded by enemy vessels, she made a daring move ramming into another Persian ship sinking it. The Greeks thought she had joined their side and stopped their attack allowing her escape.

From a nearby cliff, Xerxes watched Artemisia's ship break through the chaos. He praised her cleverness, not realizing what had truly happened, and exclaimed: 'My men have become women, and my women men!'

After the battle, Artemisia was trusted with guarding Xerxes' sons and advising him on future military plans. She proved that leadership has nothing to do with gender and everything to do with courage, intellect, and action.

Artemisia remains one of the first known female commanders in history. She was a strategist, warrior, and queen whose name still sails through time, cutting through doubt like the ships she once led.

Queen Cleopatra VII

The Last Pharaoh

Battles of Alexandria and Actium (69 BCE)

CLEOPATRA VII wasn't just a queen; she was a smart leader, a skilled speaker, and a fighter. Born in 69 BCE, Cleopatra stood out from her royal Greek family that had ruled Egypt for almost 300 years. She spoke Greek, Egyptian and nine other languages. She studied astronomy, medicine, philosophy, and how to lead in war. She believed that knowledge was power, and she used her knowledge and power to protect her people.

Cleopatra became queen at 18 when her father died, ruling with her younger brother. But enemies at court forced her to leave the palace. She didn't give up. Instead, she came back in secret, rolled up in a carpet that was delivered as a gift to the Roman general Julius Caesar. When the carpet was unwrapped, Cleopatra stepped out and spoke so wisely and bravely that Caesar helped her get her throne back. She fought with her soldiers in the Siege of Alexandria, helping to win back control of Egypt.

After Caesar's death, Cleopatra teamed up with another Roman general, Mark Antony. Unlike many others, he treated her as an equal. Together, they tried to lead the eastern part of the Roman Empire and protect Egypt from danger. Cleopatra didn't stay away from battle. She wore armor, stood beside her soldiers, and helped lead one of the largest navies in history. At the Battle of Actium in 31 BCE, she commanded her fleet from a grand warship decorated in gold. Even when the tide turned against her, Cleopatra kept fighting. But they lost.

Surrounded by the forces of Octavian, who would become Rome's first emperor, Cleopatra and Antony chose not to be captured. Cleopatra died with pride, in her own way, rather than be shown off as a prisoner. With her death, Egypt lost its independence and became part of the Roman Empire. She was the last pharaoh of ancient Egypt. Over time, some people tried to say Cleopatra only used beauty to get her way, but that's not true. She was smart, strong, and brave. Cleopatra was one of the most powerful women of the ancient world, and she fought for her people until the very end.

Trung Sisters

Dragons of Resistance

Trưng Sisters' Rebellion, Han–Vietnamese War (AD 40–43)

MORE THAN 2,000 years ago, before Vietnam had its current name, two brave sisters Trưng Trắc [choong chuhk] and Trưng Nhị [choong nyee] stood up to one of the most powerful empires in the world. They were born into a noble family while Vietnam was ruled by China's Han Dynasty. At that time, girls were expected to stay quiet and follow orders, but the Trưng Sisters were different. They learned stories of proud ancestors who had once ruled themselves, and they believed they could do it again. Their father made sure they were educated and trained in martial arts, horseback riding, and how to lead.

When a cruel Chinese official killed Trưng Trắc's husband for speaking out, the sisters decided they couldn't stay silent. They would fight back. In the year AD 40, the sisters led a rebellion. Trưng Trắc became the leader, while Trưng Nhị helped lead their army in battle. Their army grew to more than 80,000 people, many of them women. They took control of over 60 cities in northern Vietnam and ruled for three years. The Chinese emperor was angry. He sent a top general named Ma Yuan with a huge army to stop the rebellion. The sisters and their fighters were brave, but they were outnumbered.

In AD 43, their army lost. Rather than be captured, the sisters are said to have jumped into the Hát River, choosing death over defeat. Even though their rebellion ended, their bravery became a powerful symbol. Vietnamese people still honor the Trưng Sisters today. Statues, temples, and schools carry their names. They are remembered not as victims but as heroes who led their people with courage. They didn't wear crowns or hold royal titles, but they led like queens. One old story says: "All the other generals are not worth mentioning. But as for Trưng Trắc she led her people with more valor than them all." The rebellion ended long ago, but the courage of the Trưng Sisters still inspires people today.

Queen Boudica

The Fire of Freedom

The Iceni Rebellion against Rome (60–61 CE)

Boudica [BOO-dih-kah] was a queen of the Iceni, a Celtic tribe in ancient Britain. She lived during the 1st century, when the Roman Empire ruled over much of the land. Her husband, King Prasutagus, hoped to keep the peace by leaving his kingdom to both their daughters and the Roman Emperor Nero. But the Romans broke that promise. Roman soldiers stormed the Iceni lands. They took the family's property, beat Boudica in public, and assaulted her daughters. The Romans expected her to stay silent. Instead, Boudica rose.

With fire in her heart, she gathered nearby tribes to fight back. She led tens of thousands into battle. Riding in a chariot beside her daughters, she became the face of the rebellion. She wore a long flowing cloak, carried a spear, and her fierce voice carried across the army. To her people, she was more than a queen, she was a warrior sent by the gods to deliver justice.

They attacked Roman cities, burning Camulodunum (now Colchester), Londinium (London), and Verulamium (St. Albans). Historians say over 70,000 Roman citizens and soldiers were killed. The fear she spread shook Rome itself. Under London today, archaeologists have found a thick red layer of ash, proof of the destruction Boudica left behind.

Before her final battle, Boudica gave a powerful speech: "I fight not for a kingdom, but for freedom. For my bruised body. For my outraged daughters." Her warriors cheered, believing they could bring down an empire. The Romans eventually defeated her army, but her spirit never faded.

Boudica became a legend remembered not just for her fury, but for her courage. She showed the world that when justice is denied, even an empire can be shaken by the fire of one woman's fight for freedom. Statues of Boudica stand today in London, her chariot charging forward, a reminder of her strength. Her story lives on, proving that the voice of one woman can echo through the centuries.

Shieldmaiden Lagertha

Wolf of the North

The Viking Wars (800–850 CE)

LAGERTHA [IAH-GER-THAH] was a legendary warrior woman from Norway, known as a shield-maiden and one of the fiercest fighters of the Viking Age. Her story was first written down around the 12th century in the Gesta Danorum by Saxo Grammaticus, where he described her as one of the greatest of warriors.

Lagertha fought beside the famous Viking Ragnar Lothbrok. When his army was in danger, Lagertha rushed into battle, sword in hand, and fought so fiercely that many assumed she was a man until her long hair fell loose from her helmet. Saxo wrote of her: "A skilled Amazon, who, though a maiden, had the courage of a man, and fought in front among the bravest with her hair loose over her shoulders."

Her bravery changed the course of the fight and saved Ragnar's men from defeat. Some legends say Ragnar asked for her hand in marriage because of her courage, though their story did not end happily. Whether in victory or betrayal, Lagertha's name was remembered.

For a long time, people thought Lagertha was only a legend. But in the 1800s, archaeolo-gists discovered Viking graves buried with weapons, horses, and signs of military rank. These graves had been assumed to belong to men until modern DNA tests revealed that many were women. One famous grave in Birka, Sweden, held a warrior laid to rest with a sword, a spear, two horses, and full armor.

Another in Norway revealed a young woman with battle wounds and a horse at her side. We may never know who these women were, but they echo the legend of Lagertha. She could represent one of these warriors or many women like her who fought in the Viking Age. What was once dismissed as myth is now understood as truth. Women sailed longships, led warriors, and died in battle. Lagertha may have become a legend, but the strength in her story is rooted in history. Her tale reminds us that courage knows no boundary of gender, and that sometimes myth preserves the memory of truths long hidden.

Lady Æthelflæd

The Protector of Mercia

The Viking Wars of Anglo-Saxon England (870–918 CE)

ÆTHELFLÆD [ETH-EL-FLED] was a powerful ruler in early medieval England, known for her courage, leadership, and sharp mind. Over 1,100 years ago, during a time of Viking raids and political upheaval, she rose to power and helped change the course of history.

She was the daughter of King Alfred the Great, one of England's most famous rulers. Like her father, Æthelflæd believed in protecting her people from invasion. When she married the ruler of Mercia, a central English kingdom, she became more than a royal wife. She studied politics, watched battles, and learned how kingdoms were defended. After her husband died, Æthelflæd ruled Mercia in her own right, something almost no woman had ever done.

She did not rule from the shadows. Æthelflæd rode with her armies into battle, planned campaigns, and built strong fortresses called "burhs" to defend her towns. These forts became safe havens where farmers and families could gather if raiders came. With her brother, King Edward of Wessex, she fought to reclaim land from Viking control. Together, they changed the map of England.

One of her greatest victories was the capture of the Viking stronghold of Derby. Historians believe even Viking leaders respected and feared her. She was called the "Lady of the Mercians," and unlike many rulers of her time, she was loved by her people. They saw her not only as a warrior but also as a protector.

Æthelflæd also rebuilt churches, supported education, and strengthened trade. She under-stood that true leadership was not only about winning wars but also about giving her people a future worth fighting for. When she died in 918, the Mercians were so loyal that they chose her daughter to rule after her—an almost unheard-of act in those days.

Æthelflæd's legacy shows that leadership is not about titles or tradition. It is about action, courage, and care for the people you serve. She was a shield for her people and a force that shaped a nation.

Samurai Tomoe Gozen

Blade of the Rising Sun

Battle of Awazu, Genpei War (1180–1185 CE)

IN 12TH-CENTURY JAPAN, the warrior path of the samurai was meant for men—until Tomoe Gozen [toh-MOH-eh GOH-zen] changed everything. Her name means "circle," like the swirl of the tomoe crest painted on shields and armor, but her story cut straight through history.

Tomoe was no ordinary woman. From a young age, she trained in archery, horseback riding, swordsmanship, and battlefield tactics. She learned to ride swift horses across rivers, draw a bow with deadly accuracy, and fight with the curved katana sword. In a time when women were expected to stay behind walls, she prepared to ride into battle. Her skill was so great that she became a trusted commander under Minamoto no Yoshinaka, one of the most powerful generals of the Genpei War.

The Genpei War (1180-1185) was a brutal civil war between the Minamoto and Taira clans over who would rule Japan. Tomoe did not just fight, she led. Tomoe wore full armor, carried a long curved blade, and rode at the front lines beside the strongest warriors. According to The Tale of the Heike, an epic account of the war: "She was especially beautiful, with white skin, long hair, and charming features. A remarkable archer, and as a swordswoman she was worth a thousand warriors."

In 1184, at the Battle of Awazu, Tomoe's army faced defeat. Loyal to her commander until the end, she fought with fearless strength. One story says she charged into enemy lines, pulled a powerful samurai from his horse, and cut him down in a single strike. Then, she vanished from history. Some believe she died that day. Others say she became a nun, living in quiet reflection after years of war. A few legends claim she was captured, forced into marriage, and later escaped. No one knows for certain what happened to Tomoe after that final battle. What is certain is that she was real. She rode into war in a world that did not expect women to lead, and she led anyway. She is remembered not only because she was different, but because she was excellent. In a time that tried to forget her, her legend endured, inspiring generations to come.

Princess Khutulun

14

The Wrestling Princess

Battles of the Mongol Empire (1260–1306 CE)

ACROSS THE ENDLESS grasslands of 13th-century Central Asia, where warriors lived on horseback and empires rose and fell with the thunder of hooves, one name rode against the wind, Khutulun [KOO-too-loon]. She was the daughter of Kaidu Khan and cousin of Kublai Khan, born into power but determined to earn respect not as a princess, but as a warrior.

From childhood, Khutulun trained in the arts of war: horseback riding, archery, sword fighting, and Mongol wrestling. While other women of the court wore silk, she wore armor. She rode beside her father into battle, defending their lands from rivals like the Yuan dynasty. In the chaos of combat, her presence was unmistakable fast, fierce, and fearless.

Wrestling was more than a sport in Mongol culture; it was sacred. Khutulun vowed she would only marry a man who could defeat her in a wrestling match. One by one, challengers came from across the empire. All were thrown to the ground. With each victory, Khutulun claimed 100 horses. By legend, she won more than 10,000, a living ocean of hoof beats that marked her strength and reputation. But Khutulun was more than an athlete. Her father trusted her as a military advisor and, according to some accounts, wished to name her his heir. Many nobles refused to follow a woman, yet Khutulun still held great influence. She commanded troops, gave counsel in war councils, and rode at the front of armies as both leader and fighter.

Even foreign travelers like Marco Polo wrote of her, describing a warrior princess who led men into war and never lost in the wrestling ring. Centuries later, her legend may have inspired the opera Turandot, the tale of a woman who tested her suitors with impossible challenges, but Khutulun was no myth. She was a general, a champion, and a daughter of the empire who refused to be anyone's prize. She wrestled for honor. She wrestled for power. And above all, Khutulun wrestled for the right to lead and she won.

Joan of Arc

16

The Girl Who Led an Army

Siege of Orléans, Reims Campaign, and Capture at Compiègne (1400s)

IN THE 1400S, France was at war and full of fear. Then a teenage girl said she was sent by heaven to save her country. Her name was Joan of Arc.

Joan was born in 1412 in the small village of Domrémy. She grew up during the Hundred Years' War, a long and bitter struggle between France and England. Many towns were burned, families were torn apart, and the French king had not even been crowned. People were losing hope—but not Joan.

At age 13, Joan said she heard voices from saints. They told her to help the French army and make sure the rightful king, Charles VII, was crowned. At 17, she cut her hair short, put on armor, and convinced a commander to take her to meet Charles. When she spoke with him, she said she had been sent by God to lead his army. Against all odds, he believed her. Joan, still a teenager, was given troops to command.

In 1429, she helped win a great victory at the Siege of Orléans. Joan did not carry a sword— she carried a white banner painted with holy symbols. Her courage spread through the soldiers, and the French army believed they could fight again. That summer, Charles was crowned king at Reims, with Joan by his side. She had completed the mission she said God had given her.

But her story did not end in triumph. In 1430, Joan was captured by enemies of France and sold to the English. They put her on trial, not for crimes, but to silence her voice. She was accused of heresy and punished for dressing as a man. In 1431, at only 19 years old, Joan was burned at the stake.

Years later, the church admitted her trial was unjust. In 1920, Joan was declared a saint. But to the people of France, she had always been more than a soldier. She was a girl who gave them hope, a leader who showed that faith and courage could change the future of a nation. Joan once said: "I am not afraid… I was born to do this."

Countess Caterina Sforza

The Tigress of Forlì

Italian Wars (1488–1499)

IN RENAISSANCE ITALY, a time of castles, rival families, and constant battles, one woman stood out for her bravery and clever mind—Caterina Sforza [kah-teh-REE-nah SFOR-tsah]. She was born in 1463 into the powerful Sforza family, rulers of Milan. From an early age, Caterina learned about politics, survival, and strategy. She grew up in a world where betrayal could happen overnight, and she learned to use both her intelligence and her courage to survive.

As a young woman, Caterina married Girolamo Riario, the nephew of Pope Sixtus IV, and moved to the city of Forlì. Together, they ruled Forlì and nearby Imola. But in 1488, rebels killed her husband and threatened to overthrow her family.

Many expected Caterina to surrender. Instead, she shocked them all by seizing the main fortress and facing down the rebels directly, refusing to bow. One famous story says that when the rebels threatened to harm her children, she stood on the fortress walls and declared she could have more children, but she would never give up her power. Whether or not that exact detail is true, the legend captured her fearless spirit.

As ruler, Caterina was more than a political figure. She strengthened her cities' defenses, planned military strategies, and even studied science and alchemy, unusual pursuits for women of her time. When the Italian Wars broke out, she rode into battle herself, wearing armor and commanding troops.

In 1499, her greatest challenge came when Cesare Borgia, the ambitious son of the pope, attacked Forlì with a powerful army. Caterina fought back with determination, but the odds were against her. After fierce resistance, she was captured and taken to Rome. Even in defeat, she refused to show weakness.

After her release, she lived in Florence, where she continued her studies until her death in 1509. Caterina Sforza became known as the "Tigress of Forlì" because she never surrendered her pride or her strength. She proved that a woman could not only rule but also fight, standing tall among the fiercest leaders of her time.

Queen Amina

The Sword of Zazzau

Military Campaigns Across Hausaland and Beyond Nigeria, (1500s)

QUEEN AMINA OF Zazzau [ZAH-zow] was born in the 1500s in what is now northern Nigeria. Her mother, Queen Bakwa Turunku, ruled the Hausa kingdom of Zazzau, one of the great city-states of West Africa. Though raised in the royal court, Amina was drawn more to weapons than weaving. While other girls practiced traditional roles, Amina trained with swords, rode swift horses, and studied battle strategy with the warriors of her kingdom.

After her mother's death, Amina's younger brother took the throne. Many expected her to fade into the background, but Amina proved herself in combat again and again. Her courage and tactical skill earned the trust of Zazzau's army, and in 1576 she became queen not by inheritance alone, but by showing she could lead from the front lines.

For more than 30 years, Queen Amina commanded armies across West Africa. Clad in armor and mounted on a warhorse, she carried a spear and sword, and she personally led charges into battle. Under her leadership, Zazzau grew into a regional power. Her campaigns stretched the borders of her kingdom to the Niger River in the west and to the edge of the Sahara Desert in the north.

Amina was not only a warrior. She was a builder and protector. She secured trade routes that brought wealth to her people, demanded tribute from rival rulers, and fortified cities with strong defenses. Wherever her armies camped, she ordered protective walls to be built. Many of these earth packed walls still stand today and are remembered as "Amina's walls."

Unlike many rulers of her time, Amina never married. She devoted her life to warfare, diplomacy, and governance. Her people honored her not just as their queen but as their shield. Legends grew around her; some claimed she never lost a battle, others said she rode the largest horse in all of Africa or fought with two swords at once.

Even if some of these tales grew larger with time, one thing is certain: Queen Amina was a brilliant strategist and fearless warrior who reshaped her kingdom through strength, wisdom, and resolve.

Commander Grace O'Malley

The Pirate Queen

Irish Naval Commander, Tudor Wars (1500s)

THEY CALLED HER wild. Rebellious. Dangerous. To the English crown, she was a trouble-maker. But to her people, she was a queen.

Grace O'Malley was born around 1530 in western Ireland. Her family were powerful sea captains who ruled the waters of Clew Bay. They traded goods, protected their land, and sometimes raided other ships. From the time she was a little girl, Grace wanted to sail. When her father told her no, saying her long hair would get tangled in the ropes, Grace cut it all off. The sea was calling, and she wasn't going to be left behind.

By her twenties, Grace was already proving herself as a leader. After her first husband died, she took command of his ships, land, and castle. Later, she married again, but when that short union ended, she kept the castle and sent the man away. Grace lived by her own rules.

She wasn't only a sailor; she was a commander. Grace led fleets of ships, collected tolls from anyone passing through her waters, and defended her people against rivals and raiders. One famous story tells how her ship was attacked while she was giving birth. Barely an hour later, she wrapped herself in a blanket, returned to the deck, and took command, helping her crew win the battle.

As Grace's power grew, so did her enemies. The English saw her as a dangerous rebel who defied their control of Ireland. They tried to weaken her influence by seizing her family and restricting her trade, but Grace was not one to be silenced. In 1593, she sailed directly to London to meet Queen Elizabeth I. She refused to bow, spoke through a translator, and boldly demanded the release of her captured sons. Against all expectations, Elizabeth agreed.

Grace O'Malley died around 1603, the same year as Queen Elizabeth. She left behind no books or portraits, only songs, legends, and the memory of her courage. Grace was more than a pirate. She was a mother, a fighter, and a voice for her people. The sea may have been wild, but so was she, and she ruled it with fearless command.

Queen Nzinga Mbande

The Warrior Queen Who Defied Empires

Portuguese Colonial Expansion (1600–1663)

IN THE 17TH century, as European empires pushed deeper into Africa and the transatlantic slave trade tore families apart, one African queen stood her ground, brilliant, bold, and unyielding. Her name was Nzinga Mbande [en-ZEEN-gah m-BAHN-day], Queen of Ndongo and Matamba, in what is now Angola.

Nzinga was born in 1583 to the royal family of the Ndongo Kingdom. She grew up in a time of war and resistance, and her father trained her in politics, diplomacy, and the art of war. While other girls learned court manners, Nzinga practiced with spears, studied the rivalries between kingdoms, and learned how to outthink her enemies. She spoke multiple languages and was known for her sharp intellect and commanding presence. When Portuguese forces invaded Ndongo, hoping to colonize the land and enslave its people, Nzinga's brother, the king sent her to negotiate peace. At the tense meeting, the Portuguese governor refused her a chair, a deliberate insult meant to diminish her status. Nzinga refused to be humiliated. She calmly ordered a servant to kneel so she could sit, turning a cruel gesture into a bold declaration of sovereignty.

After her brother's death, Nzinga claimed the throne and became queen of both Ndongo and Matamba. She transformed into a wartime leader, forging alliances with African rivals, escaped slaves, and even the Dutch to resist Portuguese domination. She welcomed the formerly enslaved into her ranks and trained women to fight alongside men.

For nearly 40 years, Nzinga led her armies in battle. Even into her sixties and seventies, she rode into war wearing armor, spear in hand, unafraid of imperial power. In her later years, she secured peace with Portugal on favorable terms, ensuring her kingdom's survival until her death in 1663. Nzinga's reign was not only about war, it was about sovereignty, survival, and freedom. Her people remembered her not just as a queen, but as a liberator. Statues of her stand in Angola today, honoring her words and her legacy: "While I live, I will never be a slave."

Commander Begum Samru

The Mercenary Queen of India

Battles of the Mughal Empire and the Rohilla Wars (1700s)

IN 18TH-CENTURY INDIA, battles raged across the Mughal Empire as rival powers and foreign armies fought for control. Amid this chaos, a girl named Farzana [far ZAH-nah] was born in Delhi around 1750. Life was not easy, and she had to grow up quickly. As a teenager, she became a dancer in the royal courts, trained in music, poetry, and performance.

Her beauty and talent caught the attention of Walter Reinhardt, a European mercenary commander who led his own army. Reinhardt took Farzana into his household, and from there her life changed forever. While others saw her only as a companion, she was watching and learning. She studied how Reinhardt commanded troops, how he struck alliances, and how battles were won and lost.

When Reinhardt died in 1778, most expected his army to scatter. Instead, the soldiers turned to Farzana. They trusted her intelligence and her courage, and they chose her as their leader. From that moment, she became known as Begum Samru "Lady Samru." She was small in size, just four and a half feet tall, but she stood at the front of an army of thousands. She commanded five battalions of infantry, more than 300 officers, and 40 cannons. She rode into battle in armor, leading from the front, her presence sparking both loyalty in her troops and fear in her enemies. Some whispered that she used magic, but those who knew her said her real power was her sharp mind and steady leadership.

During the Rohilla Wars, Begum Samru twice defended the Mughal emperor Shah Alam in battle. For her bravery, he honored her with titles and even called her the "Daughter of the Emperor." Later, as ruler of Sardhana, she became known not only as a fighter but also as a just and wise leader. She built homes, supported widows and orphans, and ensured her people lived in peace.

Her palace still stands today, a symbol of her strength and success. Begum Samru began life far from power, yet through intelligence, bravery, and determination, she rose to become one of the most respected and feared leaders in India's history. Her story proves that true power comes not from where you start, but from how fiercely you choose to lead.

Commander Wang Cong'er

Ghost in the Wind

White Lotus Rebellion, Qing Dynasty China (1700s)

IN THE LATE 1700s, China was ruled by the Qing Empire. Life was hard for ordinary people. Farmers worked from dawn until dusk and still went hungry. Families paid heavy taxes to a government that seemed far away and uncaring. Out of this hardship, voices of resistance began to rise.

In a small village in Henan Province, a girl named Wang Cong'er [wahng tsong-ur] was born in 1777. Her family was poor, but she was strong in body and spirit. From a young age, she trained in acrobatics and martial arts. She could leap, flip, and move with incredible speed. Neighbors said she was as fast as the wind, a girl destined for something greater.

When the secretive White Lotus Society began to grow, Wang Cong'er joined them. The White Lotus followers believed injustice and equality. They promised hope to the poor and forgotten, and they dared to resist the mighty Qing dynasty. When one of the leaders was killed, many thought the rebellion would collapse. Instead, Wang Cong'er stepped forward.

She did not only plan battles she fought in them. Armed with a sword in each hand, she led an army of farmers, workers, and women who had nothing left to lose. They struck swiftly through forests and mountains, appearing and disappearing like shadows. Stories spread of her leaping over rooftops and vanishing into mist. Soon she was called the "Ghost in the Wind."

The Qing government was alarmed. They sent thousands of soldiers to crush her rebellion. Time and again, Wang Cong'er escaped using clever strategies and her deep knowledge of the land. For a while, she seemed unstoppable. But in 1798, she and her forces were finally surrounded. Refusing to be captured, Wang Cong'er chose her own fate. She leapt from a cliff, embracing freedom even in death.

Though her rebellion ended, her legend endured. Her name was whispered in secret songs, remembered in tales passed from one generation to the next. Today, Wang Cong'er is honored as a hero, a woman who fought for justice with heart, strength, and two flashing blades.

Mary Ludwig Hays

30

Molly Pitcher

Battle of Monmouth, American Revolutionary War, (1778)

MARY LUDWIG HAYS was not a soldier by rank, but during the American Revolution she became a legend. At the Battle of Monmouth, she earned the name 'Molly Pitcher,' a title given to women who carried water to soldiers fighting under the burning summer sun.

Mary had followed her husband, William Hays, who served as a gunner in the Continental Army. Like many wives of soldiers, she lived in camp, cooking meals, washing clothes, and tending to the sick and wounded. Life was hard, but Mary refused to stay behind when the army marched. She chose to be by her husband's side.

It was one of the hottest weeks on record. Soldiers collapsed from heatstroke as gunfire and cannon smoke filled the fields. Mary saw men falling, their throats parched and the cannons overheating. Without hesitation, she grabbed a pitcher of water and began running back and forth across the battlefield. Again and again, she braved enemy fire to quench the thirst of the soldiers and cool the burning cannon barrels.

Then came the moment that changed her story forever. Her husband fell beside his cannon, too weak to continue. Without pausing, Mary stepped into his place. She seized the rammer, joined the gun crew, and kept the weapon firing. Cannonballs tore through the air around her. One shot ripped through the hem of her dress. Mary looked down, saw she was unhurt, and joked that the cannonball had "missed the important parts" then went right back to loading and firing.

Some stories say General George Washington himself saw her that day and praised her bravery. After the war, Mary was awarded a small military pension in recognition of her service, something almost unheard of for a woman in her time. Mary Ludwig Hays did not set out to become a hero. She simply saw what needed to be done and stepped forward. That is why she is still remembered as Molly Pitcher the water carrier who carried courage, too.

Captain Nadezhda Durova

Nadezhda the Brave

Napoleonic Wars , Russia (1800s)

IN THE EARLY 1800s, Russia was a land of soldiers, snow, and empire. Nadezhda Durova [nah-DYEZH-dah doo-ROH-vah] was born into a military family and grew up surrounded by horses, sabers, and the steady rhythm of marching boots.

While most girls were expected to sit quietly and learn embroidery, Nadezhda wanted something more. She dreamed of of galloping across open fields and fighting for honor. Her parents tried to stop her. They took away her sword and gave her a needle. "This is what proper young ladies do," they said. But Nadezhda refused to live a quiet life. She cut her hair short, put on a cavalry uniform, and ran away from home. Disguised as a man, she called herself Alexander Sokolov and joined a regiment of the Russian army.

No one knew her secret. She rode hard, trained fiercely, and earned her place among the soldiers. During the Napoleonic Wars, a massive conflict between Russia and France, she proved her courage in battle. In her first campaign in 1807, she lost her equipment and gave up her horse to help a wounded comrade, but she stayed calm under fire. Later, she wrote, "I didn't act out of courage. I just didn't know what fear was yet."

Her bravery soon became legend. When she risked her life to rescue a fallen officer, word reached Tsar Alexander I himself. Impressed by her heroism, he awarded her the Cross of St. George, Russia's highest honor for bravery in combat. Nadezhda was the first woman in Russian history to receive it.

Eventually, her true identity was discovered. Some officers wanted her dismissed, but Nadezhda stood firm. "All I ask is to remain a soldier," she told the Tsar. He agreed. She continued to serve with honor and later became one of Russia's first published war memoirists.

Through her writing, Nadezhda gave the world a glimpse of what it meant to live as both a woman and a warrior. She wasn't pretending to be someone else, she was becoming who she always knew she was: a soldier with a fearless heart.

Admiral Laskarina Bouboulina

The Admiral Who Began Life in a Prison

Greek War of Independence, (1821–1825)

IN THE EARLY 1800s, Greece was under the control of the powerful Ottoman Empire. Many Greeks longed for freedom, and among the boldest leaders in the fight was a woman named Laskarina Bouboulina [lahs-kah-REE-nah boo-boo LEE-nah].

She was born in a prison in Constantinople after her father was jailed for supporting a failed rebellion. When he died, her mother moved their family to the island of Spetses, a place filled with sailors, merchants, and dreams of liberty.

Growing up near the sea, Laskarina felt at home on the water. She married two sea captains, and when her second husband died, she inherited his ships and his fortune. But instead of choosing a life of comfort, she chose to fight for her country's independence.

Bouboulina secretly built and armed a massive warship called the Agamemnon one of the largest vessels in the Greek fleet. When the revolution began in 1821, she raised the first Greek revolutionary flag from her ship's mast and led her fleet into battle. She helped blockade the port of Nafplio, fought in the sieges of Monemvasia and Tripolitsa, and planned daring naval missions. Her courage inspired the fighters around her, and her leadership earned respect from both soldiers and civilians.

But Bouboulina's strength was not only seen in battle. She opened her home to refugees fleeing the violence of war and helped protect women and children left homeless by the fighting. She sold her own jewelry and spent her fortune to feed and arm her people.

In 1825, Bouboulina was killed during a family dispute, an ending unworthy of her bravery. Yet Greece never forgot her. She was posthumously honored with the rare title of Admiral, one of the few women in history to hold such a rank.

Born in chains but destined for command, Laskarina Bouboulina proved that heroes are not defined by how their stories begin, but by how fiercely they fight for the freedom of others.

Lieutenant Maria Quitéria

The Iron Rebel

Brazilian War of Independence, (1820s)

IN A QUIET village in Bahia, Brazil, a young girl named Maria Quitéria de Jesus grew up with fire in her heart and courage in her hands. While other girls were taught to sew, she learned to shoot, ride horses, and hunt through the forests near her home. Her mother died when she was young, and her father expected her to live a simple life, to marry, tend the farm, and stay silent. But Maria dreamed of something greater.

When Brazil declared independence from Portugal in 1822, calls for volunteers spread across the land. Men rushed to enlist. Women were expected to wait. Maria's father forbade her from joining, insisting war was no place for a woman, but Maria refused to be left behind. She cut her hair short, borrowed her brother-in-law's uniform, and enlisted under the name José Medeiros.

She was placed in the Batalhão dos Periquitos, the "Parakeet Battalion," named for their green-feathered helmets, and sent into battle. Maria proved fearless. She fought in the trenches of Itapuã, the hills of Pituba, and the swamps near the Paraguaçu River. Her aim was sharp, her commands steady. When her father discovered her disguise and tried to have her removed, her officers refused. They had seen her bravery and promoted her instead—first to cadet, then to lieutenant.

Her story spread across the country. In 1823, Emperor Dom Pedro I summoned her to Rio de Janeiro. Standing before the emperor in full uniform, Maria was awarded the Imperial Order of the Southern Cross, Brazil's highest military honor. She became the first woman in Brazil's history to serve openly in the armed forces.

After the war, Maria returned home and lived quietly with her daughter. But her courage echoed far beyond Bahia. Today, her name is etched in Brazil's Book of Heroes and Heroines of the Fatherland. Maria Quitéria didn't wait for permission. She stepped forward when others stood still—and helped change the story of her nation.

Queen Rani Lakshmi Bai

The Queen Who Would Not Surrender

Indian Rebellion of 1857

IN 1857, A young queen in India became a symbol of resistance against British rule. Her name was Rani Lakshmi Bai [RAH-nee LUK-shmee BYE], and she stood up to one of the most powerful empires in the world.

She was born Manikarnika in 1828, in the holy city of Varanasi. Her father believed girls should learn the same skills as boys. From a young age, she trained in horseback riding, archery, and sword fighting. She was fearless, intelligent, and independent. At 14, she married the ruler of Jhansi and became queen, taking the name Lakshmi Bai.

Years later, when her husband died, the British East India Company refused to recognize her adopted son as heir. They claimed Jhansi had no rightful ruler and moved to seize the kingdom. Lakshmi Bai protested, writing letters and demanding justice, but the British ignored her. So she prepared for war.

When a widespread rebellion erupted across India in 1857, she became one of its most iconic leaders. Wearing military uniform and armor, she fought beside her soldiers, her young son strapped to her back as she rode into battle. Under siege from British forces, she refused to surrender. One British officer later said, "She was the bravest and best of the rebel leaders."

Even after Jhansi fell, she escaped on horseback and joined other rebels in Gwalior. There, she rallied her troops once more, leading them into one final fight for freedom. In June 1858, during a fierce battle, Rani Lakshmi Bai was struck down. She died with her sword still in hand-defiant to the end.

Her name became legend. Across India, statues, poems, and songs celebrate her as a warrior queen, a mother, and a national hero. Lakshmi Bai once said, "If defeated and killed on the field of battle, we shall surely earn eternal glory and salvation." She lived with honor, died with courage, and became a flame that still burns in the story of India's independence.

Dr. Mary E. Walker, MOH

The Woman with the Medal

The American Civil War (1800s)

MARY EDWARDS WALKER wasn't just a surgeon she was a rule breaker, a war hero, and a fighter in every sense. Born in 1832 in Oswego, New York, Mary grew up in a family that believed girls should be as free and educated as boys. While other young women were taught to sew and prepare for marriage, Mary studied science, wore trousers, and dreamed of becoming a doctor.

In 1855, she graduated from Syracuse Medical College, becoming one of the first female physicians in the United States. When the Civil War began six years later, Mary rushed to offer her medical skills to the Union Army. Officials told her no, women weren't allowed to serve as surgeons. But Mary didn't take no for an answer. She volunteered anyway, treating wounded soldiers in field hospitals near the front lines at Fredericksburg, Chickamauga, and Chattanooga.

Her tireless work earned her respect from the troops, and in 1863, the Army finally hired her as a contract surgeon with the 52nd Ohio Infantry. That made her the first female surgeon in U.S. Army history.

Mary refused to wear dresses in the mud and blood of battle. She designed her own version of a uniform: trousers, a short coat, and sturdy boots. Some people mocked or even arrested her for "dressing like a man." She always replied, "I don't wear men's clothes. I wear my own clothes."

One day, while treating civilians near enemy lines, Mary was captured by Confederate soldiers who believed she was a spy. She was imprisoned for four months but continued to demand supplies to care for the sick. When she was released in a prisoner exchange, the U.S. Army awarded her the Medal of Honor, the nation's highest military award.

Years later, the government tried to take it back, claiming she hadn't been an official soldier. Mary refused to return it. She wore it every day until she died at age 86. In 1977, her medal was officially restored. Mary Edwards Walker remains the only woman in history to receive the Medal of Honor, a reminder that courage doesn't depend on rank, gender, or permission. It depends on conviction.

Buffalo Calf Road Woman, Northern Cheyenne Warrior

The Girl Who Saved Her Brother

The Great Sioux War of 1876

BUFFALO CALF ROAD Woman was a Northern Cheyenne warrior who lived during a time of great danger and change in the American West. In 1874, gold was discovered in the Black Hills of South Dakota,land that had been promised to the Lakota and Cheyenne Nations through a treaty.

When settlers flooded in, the U.S. government broke its promise and demanded that Native families move onto reservations. Many refused. The Lakota, Cheyenne, and Arapaho stood together to defend their homeland.

In 1876, the tribes faced U.S. soldiers at the Battle of the Rosebud. The Lakota leader Crazy Horse led the warriors, and among them rode Buffalo Calf Road Woman. As the warriors began to pull back, her brother, Chief Comes in Sight, was shot and fell from his horse. Without hesitation, Buffalo Calf Road Woman turned her mount, charged straight through enemy fire, lifted her wounded brother onto her saddle, and carried him to safety.

Her courage sparked the fighters to return to the fray, and the Native forces drove the soldiers from the field. From that day on, the Cheyenne called it "The Fight Where the Girl Saved Her Brother."

Only days later came another clash, the Battle of the Little Bighorn, one of the most famous battles in American history. Once again, Buffalo Calf Road Woman rode into the fight, this time beside her husband and brother. According to Cheyenne oral tradition, she struck the blow that knocked General George Custer from his horse, turning the tide of battle.

Though her name was erased from most history books, her story lived on in the songs and memories of her people. To the Cheyenne, she was not just a sister or wife, she was a warrior who embodied courage, loyalty, and love.

Buffalo Calf Road Woman proved that bravery does not belong to one gender, one title, or one uniform. It belongs to those who rise in the moment when everything is on the line.

Queen Mother Yaa Asantewaa

The Queen Who Refused to Kneel

War of the Golden Stool (1900)

IN WEST AFRICA at the turn of the 20th century, a queen mother named Yaa Asantewaa [YAH ah-SAHN-teh-wah] rose to defend her people's freedom and pride. She wasn't trained as a soldier, and she didn't command from a royal throne. But when the heart of her nation was threatened, she stood tall and led her people into battle.

Born around 1840 in the town of Besease, in what is now Ghana, Yaa Asantewaa grew up in the powerful Ashanti Empire. For centuries, the Ashanti people had ruled with their own kings, culture, and traditions. By the late1800s, British colonizers had taken control of much of West Africa. They exiled the Ashanti king and demanded the Golden Stool, a sacred symbol of the Ashanti people's unity, identity, and soul.

To surrender the Golden Stool would have meant surrendering their spirit. Many male chiefs hesitated, afraid of British power. Yaa Asantewaa, the Queen Mother of Ejisu, refused to back down. Standing before the leaders, she declared, "If you, the men of Ashanti, will not go forward, then we will. We, the women, will. I shall call upon my fellow women. We will fight the white men. We will fight till the last of us falls in the battlefields."

Her words ignited a revolution. In 1900, she became the first and only woman to lead the Ashanti army in war. The conflict became known as the War of the Golden Stool. Yaa Asantewaa organized fighters, devised strategies, and led the defense of the Ashanti capital during the siege of the British fort at Kumasi. Her army was outnumbered and outgunned, but they fought with unmatched courage.

Though the British eventually captured her and sent her into exile in the Seychelles, Yaa Asantewaa's defiance became a symbol of strength for generations. She died in 1921, but her legacy still burns bright. In Ghana today, schools, festivals, and monuments bear her name. Yaa Asantewaa proved that leadership isn't given. It's claimed by those brave enough to rise when no one else will.

Major Lyudmila Pavlichenko

Lady of Death

Battles of the Eastern Front, World War II (1900s)

LYUDMILA PAVLICHENKO [lyood-MEE-lah pav-lee-CHEN-koh] was one of the most feared snipers in history. Born in Ukraine in 1916, she grew up a proud tomboy, always racing the boys, climbing trees, and proving she could do anything they could. By the time she was fourteen, she had already earned her sharpshooter badge before finishing high school. At first, she wanted to become a teacher and went to university to study history. But when Nazi Germany invaded the Soviet Union in 1941, Lyudmila knew she couldn't stay in a classroom.

She left her books behind and volunteered for the Red Army. When officials tried to assign her as a nurse, she refused. She didn't want to care for the wounded. She wanted to fight. After demanding to be tested, she outshot the men beside her and earned her place as a sniper. She became one of about 2,000 female snipers in the Soviet military, but few reached her level of skill or fame.

At the Siege of Odessa, she recorded 187 confirmed kills in just a few months. Later, at Sevastopol, she fought for eight grueling months, raising her total to 257. She even won 37 sniper duels, waiting for hours, sometimes days for the perfect shot. The Germans gave her a chilling nickname: "Lady of Death." They even broadcast messages promising to tear her into 309 pieces, one for each soldier she had killed. Lyudmila took it as proof she was doing her job well.

In 1942, shrapnel struck her face, ending her time on the front lines, but her war was not over. The Soviet government sent her abroad to speak about the fight against fascism. In the United States, she met President Franklin D. Roosevelt and First Lady Eleanor Roosevelt. During one speech, she said, "Gentlemen, I am 25 years old. I have killed 309 fascist occupants. Don't you think you've been hiding behind my back for too long?"

Her courage inspired people across the world. The American folk singer Woody Guthrie even wrote a song about her. After the war, she returned to her studies, became a historian, and lived quietly, but her legend never faded. Lyudmila Pavlichenko didn't fight for glory, she fought to defend her homeland, one bullet at a time.

588th Night Bomber Regiment

The Night Witches

588th Night Bomber Regiment, Soviet Air Force, World War II (1900s)

IN 1941, AS Nazi Germany advanced deep into Soviet territory, a famous pilot named Marina Raskova had an idea that would change history. She convinced Soviet leader Joseph Stalin to let women serve as combat pilots. From thousands of volunteers, 400 young women were chosen. Many were still in their teens. They were students, teachers, and factory workers determined to defend their homeland.

They trained fast and flew faster. Assigned to the 588th Night Bomber Regiment, they piloted small, slow biplanes made of wood and canvas. These were planes meant for training, not war. Yet these fragile machines became powerful weapons in the hands of fearless women. Flying only at night, they used paper maps and compasses to find their targets. As they approached enemy lines, they cut their engines and glided silently through the darkness, dropping bombs with deadly precision.

The Germans began to fear them, calling them the Nachthexen, the "Night Witches." To the soldiers below, the faint whoosh of their gliders sounded like broomsticks sweeping across the sky. The women flew without radios, without armor, and often without parachutes. Their cockpits were open to the freezing wind, and they wore oversized uniforms and boots that were passed down from male pilots which offered little protection. Still, they flew. Night after night, they launched up to 12 missions each, dodging bullets, searchlights, and exhaustion.

By the end of the war, the Night Witches had flown over 30,000 missions and dropped more than 23,000 tons of bombs. Twenty-three of them were awarded the title Hero of the Soviet Union, the nation's highest honor. Their regiment became the most decorated female unit in the entire Soviet Air Force.

Yet when the war ended, they were quietly disbanded, told their planes were 'too slow' to appear in the victory parade. Their speed might have been slow, but their courage soared higher than any jet. The Night Witches didn't just fight an enemy, they fought the limits placed on what women could do and proved that bravery knows no boundaries, no uniforms, and no sleep.

The Lionesses

The Lionesses

Iraq and Afghanistan, (2000s)

AFTER THE ATTACKS on September 11, 2001, the United States went to war in Iraq and Afghanistan. These battlefields were different from any before. Service members were not only fighting enemies, they were also working with local families, searching villages, and trying to build trust in places torn apart by war.

At the time, a Department of Defense policy banned women from serving in direct combat roles. Still, women often found themselves on the front lines as convoys were attacked and bases came under fire. Early in the Iraq War, some Army units began informally using female soldiers at checkpoints to search Iraqi women and children. Because of cultural and religious traditions, male troops could not touch or question women. This created blind spots, as weapons and messages were hidden among women and children.

In 2004, during the fighting in Fallujah and Ramadi, the Marine Corps formally created the Lioness Program, expanding on those early Army efforts. Women from the Marine Corps, Army, and Navy volunteered to serve as Lionesses, attached to infantry and Special Forces units on the front lines. They joined patrols and fire teams, entering dangerous neighborhoods and clearing houses alongside the men. Their mission was groundbreaking, searching women and children, gathering intelligence, and helping stop the smuggling of weapons.

The Lionesses of Fallujah became one of the first Lioness platoons and quickly proved their value. Their efforts sharply reduced the movement of explosives and weapons hidden among civilians, but their success came at a high cost. While returning from duty, their convoy was struck by an improvised explosive device (IED) in Fallujah. Several Lionesses were killed and others wounded, making them among the first female Marines lost in Operation Iraqi Freedom.

The Lionesses paved the way for Female Engagement Teams (FETs) and Cultural Support Teams (CSTs). Their legacy endures through the Women, Peace, and Security (WPS) framework, proving that courage—not gender—defines strength.

51

www.ingramcontent.com/pod-product-compliance
Lightning Source LLC
Chambersburg PA
CBRC100736150426
42811CB00070B/1915

9780998041759